T0132264

MILITARY

INDUSTRIAL COMPLEX

MEDICAL

INDUSTRIAL

COMPLEX

✳ BIO-TECHNO-TERRORIST EARA ✳

PHIEM NGUYEN

Order this book online at www.trafford.com
or email orders@trafford.com

Most Trafford titles are also available at major online book retailers.

Print information available on the last page.

ISBN: 978-1-4907-9757-1 (sc)
ISBN: 978-1-4907-9756-4 (e)

Our mission is to efficiently provide the world's finest, most comprehensive book publishing service, enabling every author to experience
success. To find out how to publish your book, your way, and have it available worldwide, visit us online at www.trafford.com

Trafford rev. 10/04/2019

www.trafford.com

North America & international
toll-free: 1 888 232 4444 (USA & Canada)
fax: 812 355 4082

MILITARY INDUSTRIAL COMPLEX
MEDICAL INDUSTRIAL COMPLEX
BIO-TECHNO-TERRORISTS
NARCISSISM

Dear Reader,

I accident lost one big part diary note and I don't have chance to prepare for my book to present diary and to show result tortured, damaged and killed evident diary.

The dangerous situation our nation and this world will face if this enslave maneuver could not be ended.

This book is summary some evidences on pictures will lead you into frightening on human rights violations, it can mark the point beginning of slave Narcissism.

No one and no Government do anything on this subject that victims and I were sent complaints to everywhere we could but hopeless solution.

Readers will be aware what will happen to you in future.

Remembered Communism created to kill, to rob, to labor, hunger death and controlled.

This Slave Narcissism is being created using High-tech Medical field to do mind control, humiliated human dignity, against people will, invaded both subconscious, physical body DIRECTED ENERGY WEAPONS, humiliated, tortured, abused, sabotaged, damaged, distracted, harmed, illness, diseases, disabled creation, deprived life and killed.

This situation can be frighten to people in this nation and the whole world will face.

I present my music describing this science research on my physical woman body and life.

I will have ebook with videos, please have it to watch DEWS(Directed Energy Weapon) attacking and songs I wrote with music but I am not musician, only one Professional produced please listen.

Phiem Nguyen
August 22, 2019
State College PA

MILITARY INDUSTRIAL COMPLEX
MEDICAL INDUSTRIAL COMPLEX
BIO-TECHNO-TERRORISTS
NARCISSISM

COMPLAINT

WHO RESPONSIBILITY?

USA, CHINA, TAIWAN, ISRAEL, ROCKEFELLER, MILITARY INDUSTRIAL COMPLEX, MEDICAL INDUSTRIAL COMPLEX

My letter to CIA

June 12, 2019

Dear CIA Director:

I would like to introduce myself to you, I am Vietnamese American, I fled out Viet Nam when Saigon surrendered to North Viet Nam in 1975, I resident in New Orleans, after Katrina hurricane I moved to Houston then sold house, moved to Horizon City, El Paso then sold house moved to Pennsylvania live with my son because lost from bought house, sold and moved several times, Targeted Individual.
I am a victim of Targeted Individual I just knew this after August 2010.
I was in fearfully, frighten and frustrated.
CIA in your profile or portfolio please let me know why I became target? Who I am? What fate, operation I was bad luck swift into that.

CIA DESTROYED MY ENTIRE LIFE!

At my age what reason CIA DESTROYED ME?
That operation continuing to my teenager then followed me until today.
I was under CIA secret research against my will, humiliated, tortured, mental terrible abused, killed, my health was paralyzed for 14 years, deprived life.
Since 2004 until today CIA used DEWs attacked to my brain, both subconscious, my woman body, my organs entire my physical body.
These technology damaged my beauty, my woman body, damaged my teeth, malfunction my organ system, harassed, high tech rape, disabled, illness, disease creation, harmful doing day and night.
Mind control sex terrible abused, neuro researched and applied control and robotized.
Perpetrators I saw Chinese and heard they were talking, who hired them or they joining research with CIA, NSA, Rockefeller.
I sent my complaint to CIA today the last one, I sent my complaint to NSA, Homeland Security, FBI, and Civil Court and Air-Force I requested investigation and settlement.

CIA responsibility for your wand of my fate life, please solve the amoral researched was burden on my life, my reputation, my life, health, my uniqueness, woman beauty and woman body, CIA pay settlements, stop TORTURE and SURVEILLANCE and official apology to me.

I am waiting for your solving this inhumanity research and atrocity crime applied research on me as Targeted Individuals.

Please investigate.

Respectfully,

Phiem Nguyen

Videos and pictures Technology attacked to me are presented below.

5G with nucleus

Organic smell but concealed something like nano nucleus can kill immediately through G5 delivered.

Silent secret scalar or nuclear highest speed kill instantly.

Laser pins with G5 delivered shot through mouth billion attacked laser pins inside mouth and throat.

Their technology weapons shot and went inside my heart to create heart failure.

Their technology weapons attacked on my head and went inside my brain to block and to create stroke.

Their technology weapons attacked to my heart and invaded inside my heart to created heart attack.

Their invisible technology weapon and their hidden hands were freely to do what they wanted to on my head, brain and my entire woman physical body.

How can I fight them back?

Government don't do anything to stop, my body was continuing along their technology weapons developed to torture, damaged, harmed and assassined.

THESE PICTURES AND VIDEOS BELOW PROVED INVISIBLE WEAPONS COULD NOT SEE WITH HUMAN EYES BUT CAMERA CAPTURED IT INTO VIDEOS AND PICTURES TO SHOW THESE TECHNOLOGY WEAPONS FROM DIRECTED ENERGY WEAPONS, SCALAR WEAPONS, NANO WIRES, NANO WEAPONS, MICROWAVE, PLASMA, ELECTRO MAGNETIC PULSE AND G5, THOSE WEAPONS AND TECHNOLOGY ATTACKED TO MY HEAD, EARS, FEMALE, RECTUM AND ENTERE BODY DURING TIME I WAS INSIDE MY HOUSE AND INSIDE MY BEDROOM,TORTURED, HARASSED, HIGH-TECH RAPED, HARMED, ABNORMAL, MALFUNCTION, ILLNESS, DISEASES, DISABLED CREATION, MIND CONTROL, MIND CONTROL SEX, ROBOTIZED NEURO RESEARCHED AND APPLIED.

TERRIBLE TORTURED AND HUMILIATED.

DAY AND NIGHT!

THESE PICTURES BELOW REPORTED THE RESULT OF NARCISSISM WERE DONE ON ME BY BIO-TECHNO-TERRORISTS

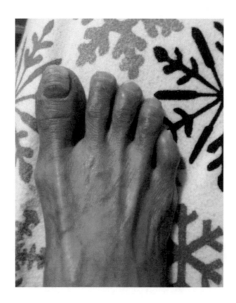

MY TOE WAS DAMAGED FROM BIO-TECHNO-TERRORISTS SHOT TO IT DURING TIME I WAS SLEEPING,TERRIBLE HURT WOKE ME UP AND FOR WEEK THEN MY TOES DAMAGED, HOW EVIL THEY ARE?

THEY DAMAGED ALL MY TEETH, MY TEETH WERE CROWN, I JUST LEFT DENTIST OFFICE THE NIGHT AFTER THEIR EMP(electro magnetic pulse)BLASTED TO MY MOUTH, THE NEXT MORNING I BRUSHED MY TEETH I COULD FEEL THE BRUSH LINES ON MY FRONT TEETH FOLLOWING THAT DAY MY TEETH DECAYED.

I WAS SO ANGRY I SAID THEY HAVE TO GROW MY NEW TEETH.

LATER THEY CUT MY MEAT BITE TEETH

RECENTLY 2019 THEY DACAYED MY NEXT TEETH FRONT OF CUTTING TEETH.

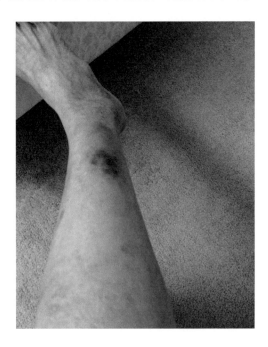

    MY LEG WAS HARMED, THEY CREATED DISEASE.
    THEY WERE CONSTANTLY HARMED MY LEGS.
    THEIR WEAPON SHOOT TO MY FEET UNDER MY SOLE HURT THEN DAY LATER DEVELOPED PAIN THEN TERRIBLE PAIN, THEY CREATED DISABLED, CANCER.
    MY LEG IN PICTURE WAS THEIR DISEASE CREATION LIKE CANCER RAPID DEVELOPED.

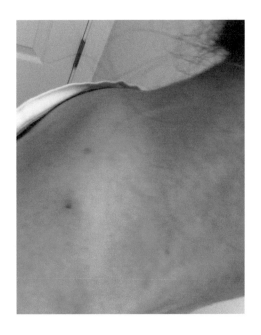

    MY BACK NECK AND SHOULDER WERE ATTACKING, THEY TRIED TO HARM MY BRAIN AND NERVES AND NERVOUS SYSTEM, I GOT DIZZINESS, UNBALANCE.
    RECENTLY 2019 THEY VIBRATED MY SHOULDER BACK AND LUNGS, 2008-2012 THEIR WEAPONS VIBRATED MY SPINE CORP(BACK BONE).

MY NECK THEIR WEAPON INSERTED INSIDE MY THOAT AND IMPLANTED CHIP, MATERIAL TRIED TO CHANGE MY VOICE, I WAS IN DIFFICULT TO TALK, I DON'T KNOW WHAT CAUSE THEY DID IT.

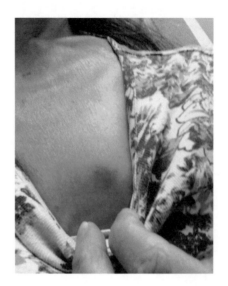

THIS IS THEIR DROLE ATTACHED TO MY HEART DURING TIME I WAS SLEEPING.

MY HEART THEY SHOT FROM MY BACK LUNG, THEIR WEAPON TOUCHED INSIDE MY HEART THEN THEIR MICROWAVE HEATED MY HEART AND UNDER MY BREASTS AND MY SIDE HEART ALL NIGHT, MY HEART WAS TIRED, I WAS TIRED, EACH TIME I GET UP OR LYING DOWN TERRIBLE HURT PAIN, THEY KILLED ME.

I SAID, THEY KNEW THEY DID TERRIBLE WRONG, THEY STOP, THEY CHANGE AND I WAS WAITING.

UNFORTUNATELY,

THAT WAS THEY DID THAT TO ME, THEY LET ME KNOW THAT THEY KILLED ME NOT CHANGE AND NOT STOP.

I SOLD MY HOUSE TO MOVE TO ANOTHER PLACE AGAIN, I WAS SILENT BECAUSE I DON'T WANT THEY COME TO DO TO PEOPLE BUT THEY CAME TO CONTINUE.

I WAS SO ANGRY, THIS TIME IS FINALE, AT ANY WAY AND ANY PRICE THEY HAVE TO BE ENDED.

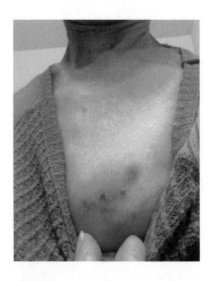

THEIR WEAPONS SHOOT TO MY HEART DURING TIME TALKING ON PHONE. MY HEART WAS EFFECTED, TIRED.

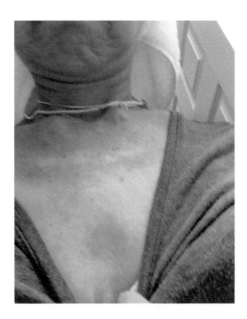

HARMED MY CENTER CHEST

SEPTEMBER 13, 2019

THEIR WEPONS SHOT UNDERMY LEFT BREAST WENT TO INSIDE MY HEART I COULD NOT EXPLAIN THE STRANGE TO MY HEART WAS EFFECTED AND IT WENT TO MY LUNG AND MY BACK, MY LUNG BACK PAINFUL, I GOT HEART FAILURE, MY HEART BEATED AND I WAS TIRE, MY HEART IN VULNERABLE CONDITION, I HAD TO TAKE THERAPY.
I TOOK PICTURES TO SHOW
THEY TRIED TO KILL ME SEVERAL TIMES.

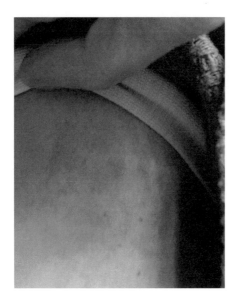

THEIR WEAPONS SHOT TO MY RIB I DON'T KNOW WHAT THEY WANTED TO DAMAGE MY HEART CASE AND ORGANS, I WAS IN TERRIBLE HURT PAIN, SEVERE, HEART WAS EFFECTED TIRED.

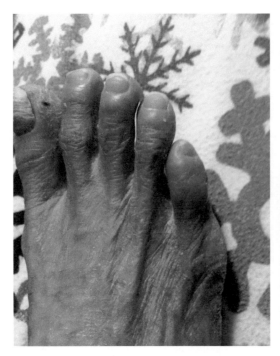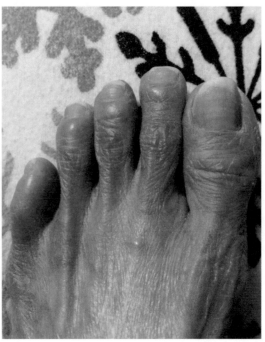

MICROWAVE BURNED AND SCALAR WEAPON ATTACKED MY LEGS AND FEET AT NIGHT INSIDE MY BED IN AWAKE AND DURING TIME I WAS SLEEPING.

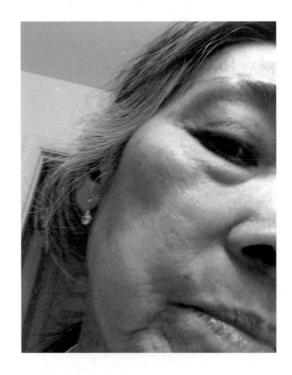

MY LIPS AND MY MOUTH THEY WERE CONSTANTLY DAMAGED, DISTRACTED SINCE 2006 UNTIL TODAY 2019.

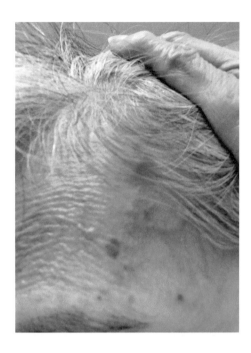

MY HEAD THEIR WEAPONS ATTACKED TO MY HEAD HURTFUL PAINFUL FOR DAYS, THEIR WEAPONS RESHAPED MY SKULL HEAD, THEY HARMED MY BRAIN, CREATED STROKE.

ALL NIGHT INVADED MY BRAIN HARMFUL DOING AND MIND CONTROL AND INSERTED THEIR DREAMS, RESEARCH ROBOT, NUERO RESEARCH AND APPLIED, PAIN, ALZHEIMER, ILLNESS CREATION FROM BRAIN.

HARASSED AND URINED SEX.

THEIR TECH FORCED WATER OUT.

THEY MALFUNCTION ABNORMAL MY URINE SYSTEM AND MY BOWEL MOVEMENT TO TORTURE ME BY THEIR CHIPS AND MATERIALS IRRITATED MY FEMALE AND RECTUM TO GO TO BATHROOM MANY TIMES THEY SET.

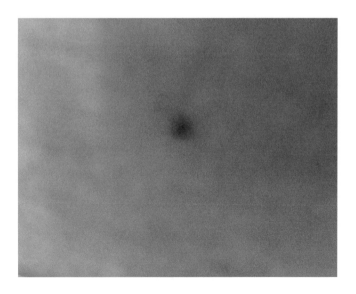

RECENTLY 2019 THEIR WEAPONS SHOT TO MY LOWER ABDOMEN, FROM THAT POINT THEY REMOTE CHURN MY BOWEL MOVEMENT.

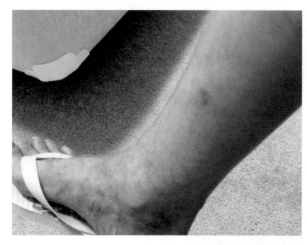 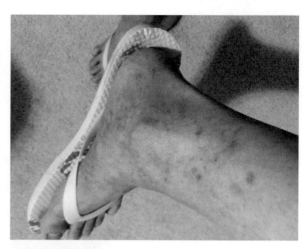

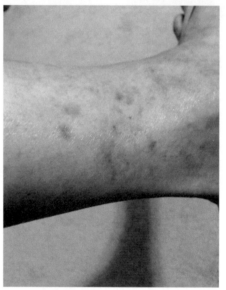

MY LEGS AND FEET WERE CONSTANTLY UNDER THEIR SCALAR AND LASER WEAPONS ATTACKING.

DISTRACTED MY LEGS, DISEASED MY LEGS, HARMED MY LEG VEINS AND NERVES, HARMED MY ORGANS FROM FEET AND SOLE, SPECIALLY MIND CONTROL FROM FEET.

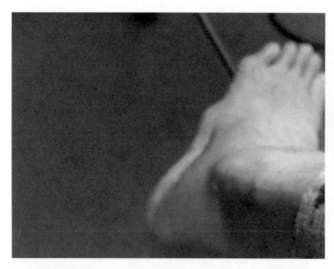 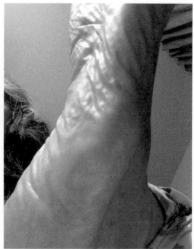

MY FEET AND SOLE ALL NIGHT WERE HARMED BY THEIR WEAPONS, MY FEET DENTED IN AND MY SOLE HAD CONE.
MY HIP WALKING JOIN BONES WERE HARMED, THEY TRIED TO HARM MY WALKING.

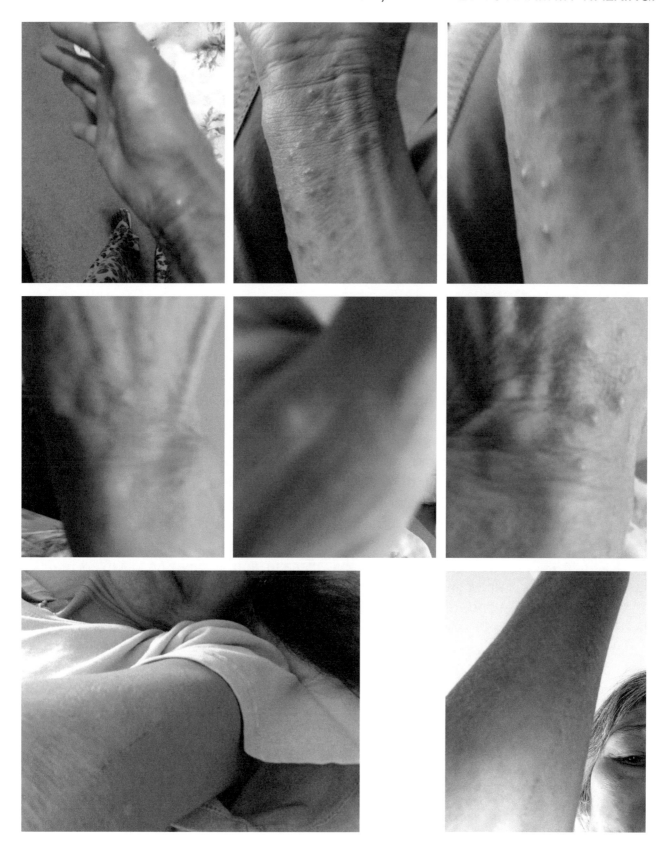

MORGELLONS AND CHICKEN POX CREATION

THEY LET DIRTY WATER TO INFECTION AND DISEASES THEN INJECTED DISEASE THEN VACCINE DISEASES.
THEY DID THESE THINGS SINCE 2010 UNTIL TODAY 2019.

Dear reader,

I suppose to have videos on my e-book but publisher said unavailable for videos on e-book.
I add some my diary into this book, readers have more information to know the torture applied each day since 2004 on physical body and brain researched and abused humiliation.

June 12, 2018

Yesterday their material at my neck two new more implanted into my neck then natural remedy loose it out then blood ran out.

What they tried to do to my neck?
I took pictures to prove.
Before yesterday they shot fiercely to my right lung during the time I took shower.
They attacked their weapon to my cheeks, I applied natural remedy terrible soar to both places, they created morgellon disease to damage my face skin.
My both sides Intestines they constantly attacked to it places to harm my health, I felt hurt for days then I saw their weapon inside my stomach like the side of drinking straw four to five inches.
At my kitchen they shot to my heart and center of my chest and constantly attacked to my neck and my mouth, my upper lip, they damaged my lip, my beauty.
I have to shield my body but I have jtwo hands for working, interrupted my working, anger creation and build up day by day for decades, how I can live under this humiliation, abused, destroyed life then now tortured, damaged, sabotaged, distracted, degraded, murdered, harass, high tech raped, malfunction organs, disease and illness and disabled creation, assassinated from their technology weapon.
Last night I was in bed, my left foot was injury by myself, they still attacking to my legs then harass my female.
I was so angry.
I could not believe human like that, cold blood and patiently, meticulous to harm people, to fell people, to suffering people to destroy people for their pleasure!
My whole life!

June 16, 2018

They attacked to my left side head, it made my brain Injury, I felt soar and something was not normal inside my brain! their weapon bombarded into my left side ear from decades, made damaged my ear and now they implanted chips to my neck then now they damaged my brain, their technology weapons created cancer to my brain, their weapons attacked to my health and entire my physical body.

They focus on my neck created cancer or something harmful to my neck and inside my throat.

Inside bathroom when I took shower, their Weapons attacked to my backbone under my belly, I felt hurt and hot to my entire back bone.

Now at this moment they attacked to my left side back head and my heart.

I am resentful

I am frustrated they never give up.

June 17, 2018

Last night I was in bed their weapon attacked to my female, first at my uterus route then to my female side, I was so angry to cried out loud.

They should be arrested, why don't arrest them?

They are real rapist, real pedophil, created sex, sick sex, incest.

They deep shot into my right lung, they harmed my health.

My lip, mouth constantly attacked to distract and damage, they harmed my old age with this mouth, chin appearance(superstition).

My face their weapon shot to my left cheek through to inside my mouth to my upper teeth.

My cheeks were microwave swollen, I took pictures to show.

My left leg their weapon injected disease or they harmed my blood and tissues to form disease, what disease this called, people and I have to ask them, cancer cell creation on my legs?

I took pictures to show my right leg and my left leg.

This is my right leg they harmed for years turn it cells to cancer cell and spread rapidly to the larger disease and damaged.

This is my left leg their weapon attacked to my left leg two days ago they formed big hard ball at my left leg and green bruise color, today it turned into brown red.

They created disease!

June 17, 2018

Last night they inserted dream or dreamed somebody dream but at the end dream they woke me up to remember my nude body in the dream afraid of like we do.

They merging subconscious?

What they tried to do mind control?

Today they attacked to my legs with their laser, shot to both legs up to thigh near female down to my toe, they harmed my walking!

I am so angry, they harmed my legs.

They attacked to my head, who harmed to my head.

June 19, 2018

They stroke to my right side neck, they harmed my vein neck after that my vein neck hurt when I used my hand to work.

My left side neck their materials implanted to my neck then they remote it to my brain I felt soar inside my brain and brain fluid, they created cancer.

They are constantly stroked to my neck these months whenever I stood at kitchen sink to do my work there.

This morning I heard noise outside my house I was busy working, I heard two men perpetrators voices I thought they came to remove their devices to attacked me but they attacked to my left side head, this weapon affected inside my brain, they knew it what was happened to my brain?

After I finished my work and took shower, they attacked to my chest, my right side breast.

After shower I went out to take trash can in, I looked to my house to see what they did to my house, I don't see, just a little piece open at my roof near the back yard porch.

Yesterday after I finished vacuumed my upper floor I took shower, I just stepped into bath tub I felt the jetted wave swept to my right leg, I was immediately felt my leg was exhausted then terrible pain I could not bear, this kind of weapon attacked to my leg several times when I was in bed.

Last night I was in bed their weapon attacked to my arms, wrists, fingers, legs, knees, ankle, feet to create pain.

This morning I vacuumed my stairs and downstairs floor, I felt hurt, pain.

They are devil actions like that to abuse me for decades, it was not easy to do my own work without single cent earn!

They are so terrible, bad luck to me and others, bad luck to this world and this mankind.

June 20, 2018

They created throat cancer to my neck, for months they constantly strokes their weapons to my neck and under mouth and chin, I could not believe these devils, this afternoon I stood at kitchen to do my work they let me inhale their chemical I smelt it was like smoke or tabaco smock. I felt soar to my neck where their weapons stroke!

They created throat cancer to my neck?

They stroked their weapons to my neck at the kitchen sink and in my bed, I took picture to show I shield my neck but they continued attacking to my neck, how devil they are?

They are devil and did what they wanted to do to victims like me!

Last night they assaulted shot their weapon to my right underarm and arm hurtful, they tried to harm my arm then attacked to my right breast to create cancer?

They create bowel movement malfunction system then control it by attacking their weapon inside my rectum, outside nerve rectum, stroked my stomach, head nerve and skin nerves to move my wast out.

They created lung problem by attacking to my both lungs!

My heart tried to kill, created heart problem!

My teeth damaged!

My bone harmed!

My leg created disease?

My skin created morgellon!

My vein shot to it to harm for years twisted vein and leg cramp!

My toes nail damaged like that, now they attacked to it!
They never stop.

June 21, 2018

Yesterday they shot deep inside my left side mouth, I felt so hurt and pain,now when I swallow I felt uncomfortable to my throat, they attacked to my under mouth and under chin at my throat, they tried to create my throat cancer by their weapons.
Today they attacked to my left side head hurtful painful, inside my brain.
I knew these are Chinese!
Daily routine attacking to my head, ears. stomach. female, eyes, bone, legs, skin diseases.
Their weapon attacked to my arm it was hurt into arm bone!
How to kill them?
These criminal devils?

June 23, 2018

Last night they attacked to my left side foot during the time I was sleeping, terrible hurt and pain from there weapon twittered my toes vein and foot and micro burned inside my flesh, bone.
This horrible hurt woke me up.
Tortured me, how I proved this tortured CIA?
Don't need to write daily attacking to my brain and physical body!

June 24, 2018

They blocked my memory, they are so terrible!
Last night I heard voices several groups were waiting for me to go to sleep in order they eat me!
But I can not try to be awaken through night because technician will instal my internet morning, I have to sleep.
This morning I woke up I knew they did something to my female, I felt different and light, they stole out my female flesh?
Recently they regularly snoozed to my female.
I saw this strange thing beside my mattress floor I don't know what it was, it was like electric cord composer, where they place this thing inside my body to snooze my female? I took pictures to show .
This evening at my kitchen sink they attacked to my female, they snoozed my female and they remote my urine poured out.
Men tortured my female for decades, now wemen attacked to my female for their pleasure, how I proved this evidence CIA?
I knew these people from Chinese.

June 25, 2018

Today I called police came to my house opened the front door for me because it was unopened. I knew this from perpetrators, they used electronic to lock my door, this is the bad situation.

They locked my door several times, they let me know they can locked my door, at that point they knew what I mention?

I was so up set?

They control door this is not the first time, several before, I noticed it but I did not say this subject until

today to call Police.

Police is so night. I Thank you so much Police officer .

Don't need to write daily routine attacked me from head to toes and from inside to skin.

They mind control and devise to make me sleeping whenever I turned on my iPhone they remote sleeping right away.

Anger each day!

June 26, 2018

Devil changed my voice, today I heard my voice was different, that what they did to my neck, throat.

What they did to my eye brows I saw and felt their weapon corn implanted to that place.

Chinese, China, Taiwan conquered they killed my ancestors to steal our Viet Nam land.

They are so terrible, they are conquerors, they created enemy almost my whole life and manipulated others did humiliate, harmed, deprived, killed, assasined, damaged, sabotaged, distracted, destroyed me but I don't know, I just knew recently.

May 12, 2019

They continued attack to my female, they used their plasma weapon to cut my female at the center my female form, what they intended to do, to form man shape on my female?

I wanted they answer me and all victims on public debate:

Why they don't do research on themselves, they will know better than on people .

They needed gay they do for themselves, they needed lesbians they do for themselves, they needed heretical sexual they create for themselves.

Why they secretly held down people head and did what they wanted to do then they said people did it, they did not do it.

I advocate nature respected that is not I am should be gay, I am should be lesbian.

They tried to transform my woman body to man.

My mental they tried to create man, lesbian, people should be pay attention on children they against people will to abuse people to nurture their sick sex, their amoral sex.

This morning they attacked to my both thigh vein.

They created and control veins.

My ears and my female assaulted attacking.

My head all night inserted their dreams to do mind control.

My female all night urine raped.

Attacked to my right side breast, attacked to my center chest.
I hate so much these devils.

May 14, 2019

Last night I was in bed began into sleeping I heard two men at my left side they caught my resting which people can say soul or spirit to float out my mind, it woke me up.

I could feel and heard many group of people surrounding me, what they tried to do during my sleeping time?

They attacked to my head pain down to my neck and arm.

They shot to my stomach hurtful they try to make stomach ache, they shot to my left side intestine painful.

Harassed my female, attacked to my ears to do mind control.

This morning attacked to my legs, feet.

Dirty water, they let me use dirty water I had stomach problem, my stomach not normal.

This morning dirty water also.

These criminals, these devils conquerors.

This evening attacked to my head, my legs, feet.

My female their weapons raped at my uterus

May 15, 2019

I hate these Chinese China conquerors and Democrat sick atrocity narcissist

They are here to target me, biowarfair from mossad, Rockfelker.

Dirty water to create diseases, cancer? Skin diseases, morgellons, and vaccine morgellons.

Where ever I moved they were moving along, dirty water the first thing to them line up DEWS and so on.

During time I was sleeping harmed my head, harmed my stomach, shot to my rib bone, shot to my intestine in my back painful, harmed my finger bone, harmed my buttercup bone.

I hate so much these conquer people.

This morning assaulted attacked to my ear to do mind control when I was in bathroom shower time.

During the day their daily routine attacked to my female. legs, feet.

This evening they attacked to my head, leg, feet, female.

Their electro microwave attacked to my entire head painful inside my mainframe when I was in bathroom.

They also attacked to my right side heart bosom and right heart rib side.

May 18, 2019

This morning I came to kitchen they attacked to my head I felt something to my head and dizziness feeling, this is microwave frequency attacking they regularly attacking to my head, I don't feel shot but the effect feeling only.

Real holocaust!

May 19, 2019

After they entered my bedroom they did something inside my uterine system then they remote water pouring out. On Facebook victim did research on this, she posted they remote water pouring out.

Mind control and nerves system to control.

Daily routine attacking don't need to write.

Attacking to my right chest to harm my heart, attacked to my eyebrows to harm my heart, chip at my eye brow to harm my heart.

Shot to my heart assassined, attacked to my female, nerves at my female tortured and harmed.

May 20, 2019

Yesterday I took nap because the night before I was interrupted sleeping, their weapon attacked to my both cheekbone, when I wash my face soaring at that place I could feel pin at my cheekbone.

This morning I washed my face I felt hurt pain at my left side end eye bone, what they did to my eye and my eye bone?

My right side end I saw darken color.

This morning I took shower they attacked to my ot near head and neck, they shot to it place it effected to inside my head then their microwave weapon or what kind of weapon attacked to my front head effected my whole head again.

They attacked to my head when I was at kitchen like laser shot my entire front head.

This afternoon inside my bedroom, they attacked to my stomach, they shot to my stomach then I sat at chair to avoid their shot they attacked inside my stomach hurtful painful, I went outside my bedroom to avoid their attacking, they waited and knew at that time I will sat at that chair inside my bedroom.'

Now at midnight I was inside my bedroom they assaulted attack to my top of my female form like the kind they attacked to my ears to do mind control.

They assaulted attack to my ear when I lied down in bed to rest.

They attacked to my head, eye lids, ears. stomach, back, arms, legs, female, rectum their daily routine.

It is past midnight I could hear they are several groups waiting for doing something or they did something during the time I was sleeping.

May 21, 2019

Their plasma weapon cut to my center female form and cut beside my back rectum, what they tried to do?

They cut at my spine cord, what they tried to do?

They shot to my top head.

They attacked to my eye brows to distracted my beauty and harmed my heart.

My thigh attacked to it to harm my thigh walking bones, why they are evil, devil? They are conquerors that is it, they tried to destroy us all.

Sick rapist and pedophile saw my nude everyday shower and toilet,

Why sick?

May 22, 2019

- [x] These Chinese conquerors and Mossad just assassined me, I sat at kitchen had meal, they shot to my two sides back head near neck and ears, they made dizziness me, killed? what they will say?

- [] This is not first time, they were constantly attacked to my back head near neck and ears, they made me dizziness several days I could not back to normal exercise my head since the night they assaulted attacked to my back head, they continued attacked to my head.

- [] My heart they attacked to my heart, just this afternoon painful at my under right breast I was busy with my hand I could not shield, I felt dizziness.

- [x] They assassined me with their technology.

May 23, 2019

They shot to my head then assaulted deep shot into my head. They continued attacking me whole day, my front head, top head, back head, ot back head near neck they tried to created stroke.

They did it, assassined me.

This morning I found out they did something like vaccine line at my back, I tried to picture it but it was not successful. What they tried to do? Created skin disease? They did it to me when I was in Houston, few days later my thigh skin were shingle disease on.

They are devils like that.

My ears constantly assaulted to do mind control.

Their weapons shot to my stomach hurt painful.

Their weapon attacked to my female day and night.

Organic smell but harmful chemical they intended to kill.

When I was in bed their stealth weapon attacked to my female.,

May 24, 2019

They continued attacking me, they shot on my head and back head and my stomach at kitchen and at kitchen sink they shot to my top head and my head.

Now I sat at chair inside my bedroom they used their stealth weapon to attacked me, their weapon attacked to my hands, my hip and my feet.

Inside bathroom they attacked to my arms and outside they usually attacked to my arms.

May 27, 2019

Recently they mind control sleeping from my phone, each time I turned on phone I read some then could not resisted sleeping.

They continue attacking to my head, back head at my neck near ears, my stomach organ and rib, my buttock bones attacked to it when I took shower, thigh nerves, feet nerves(they tried to harm my walking) my feet they tried to injected diseases.

Attacked to my female to do mind control sex.

May 28, 2019

They mind control me sleeping whenever I turned on phone to read.

They attacked me from phone also.

These conquerors.

They attacked me on my head to my brain.

They assassined me, they attacked to my ears, they attacked to my female created and remote sex.

They attacked to my feet, leg, knee bone.

They attacked to my stomach when I took shower.

Few days ago I saw the logo on my phone locked but I don't know this is hacker logo or from T-Mobile service but they hacked into my phone to attack me and stole email I save to use later.

My phone like market place.

May 30, 2019

They attacked to my ear bone connected to my head two days ago, my entire area head and neck down to my arm my back injury pain, it was call killing me with stroke they created then at my kitchen they created dizziness.

Then today they attacked to my right bone ear like they did two days ago to my left side ear bone.

My eye brown attacked to it, to harm my heart and my beauty.

My ears constantly attacked to it to do mind control.

My female constantly attacked, high-tech raped and harmed.

My head. buttock my legs were attacking.

June 3, 2019

Recently they have new weapons, with this weapon they attacked to inside my house then now they shoot their weapons to inside my mouth to harm, to kill, they might apply G5, people be aware of these kind oweapons

They kept mind control sleeping, every time I was on my phone read some I started sleeping.

Attacked to my female created urine sex I was hurry up went to bathroom with their force pouring down water.

I hate so much this technology manipulated my urine system.

They harass and raped and misshaped my female and malfunction my urine system and bowel system since 2008 until today to torture, abuse me.

Everyday is in anger motion since 2005.

They are evils, devils, I could not I imagine that kind of people!

Don't need to write down their attacking, that is their daily routine attacking me from my head, ears. neck, chest, stomach, shoulder bones, legs. Knee, feet, toes.

My nose my lip harmful doing, they believed Fansui poeple appearance, they tried to change shape my nose to be ugly and to be poor.

I was so angry, I said, if they wanted me to be poorer, they don't need to follow me to rob, to scam, to steal, and than to lie to manipulate hatred, I could not earn a single cent since 1979 today is 2019, why they wanted me to be poor? They are rich people.

They are conquerors.

June 4, 2019

I just heard their electronic sound inside house, who they are? What they did to my body last night?

This morning I sat at toilet I felt hurt pain to my female sensitive place, what they did to my female sensitive?

Jew Mossad did it or Chinese conquerors did it?

I wanted to destroy these technology target, raped, harass, sabotaged, damaged, assassin, disease, illness, malfunction, they did what they wanted to do on my body, brain, both subconscious and life.

This morning when I was inside bedroom, I saw the shadow past my bedroom door that could be some one hidden inside house they wore special material clothes, my eyes just saw shadow, I had this experience several times when I had lived in Horizon City, El Paso, I saw shadow was walking on my side walk, another time construction built houses in-front of my house, the day I went out to go to store, I saw the temporary bathroom door open but don't see human and don't see shadow, I was scare to go down that street, I turned to another street, this could be the same people in El Paso did this thing, I knew for sure this is it.

They used their painray weapon or their new kind weapon to attacked to my heart place, the whole chest under their painray shotgun, this is 5G weapon.

After heart they attacked to my stomach with their 5G painray shotgun, they were laughing when they attacking me.

June 6, 2019

They attacked to my right side under breast, their weapon shot to that place hurtful painful for continuous days and yesterday they still shot to it, they harmed my heart and killed.

Heir night they attacked to my legs bone and arm bones their weapon posed to my bones for so long to harm my bones, what they tried to do to my leg bones and arm bones? their weapon attacked to my feet and toes, attacked to my female. Heir they attacked to my head, left head hurtful painful the whole day and night.

They vaccine their skin disease at my back, they used their weapon to transmit disease on my back skin, they let me used toilet water to harm my skin, my health, crated cancer from dirty water.

They always tortured, today their weapon attacked to my head, female, stomach, left under abdomen, thighs, legs, feet.

My left knee kept attacking during time I do dishes then they shot deep big shot to my left knee, I heart the strange sound like got through the electronic barriers shaking environment in the house.

They continue attacking.

June 7, 2019

This morning attacked to my female inside bathroom, my feet.

At kitchen attacked to my ears, stomach sides, chest, back right shoulder arm bone, legs, feet.

At kitchen table attacked to my head, back neck and my back.

June 10, 2019

Hire night they attacked to my whole body painful, what their weapon was attacking me I don't know.

Their weapon attacked to my back shoulder bone harmful to my arm moving painful.

They always created pain, illness, diseases.

Last night they tortured my subconscious and urine sex all time during I was sleeping, they did mind control robot, they forced my urine out, they deformed my urine route, they damaged my urine system, they malfunction my urine system to torture me.

They woke me up three times to go to bathroom in hurry water pouring out.

They don't do anything I slept the whole night I did not go to bathroom, I woke up I was not hurry to go to bathroom.

They are sick people did ill things to people.

Their weapons attacking my legs, my feet, it was scalar weapon attacking me.

Their weapons bunch of laser shot to my stomach, they laser shot to my stomach again when I took shower, then spratch laser shot to my stomach before I ate lunch then dinner time again, harmful doing to my health.

I was so angry.

It is 11:18 p m, I was afraid sleeping because I heard soft noise inside my room and their technology vibration my bed, that meant they will do something to my body this night, I turned on light to check my room again, nothing strange or human inside my room, I wrote down this into my diary.

I wrote to here I head the noise another room or it from neighbor, I don't believe it was from neighbor.

The night they did same thing like tonight, I was sleepy could not resist, they did something inside my urine system and uterus, I don't know the new mushroom had that smell.

They shot to my left feet sole pain inside my bone feet.

Kill them if they are inside my room.

June 11, 2019

It is 3:21 a.m.

I just sent email to President of United States Donal Trump, I sent this link Total DNA Mind Control I read this article on Twitter hopefully President read it and solve this totally control human, enslave human.

it I have to be awaken I searched email to send to President, hope President Trump will stop, ban it.

When President Obama in White House I email two times and I posted on face book two times but it is continuing until today.

People said President don't have time to read.

After I sent email to President they shot to my right side ear hurt painful inside my brain, I was so angry, when they die they stop, their technology destroyed they stop, they never stop.

June 12, 2019

This night I wrote letter to send to CIA, CIA and Science did these terrible thing to my life, this is letter I email to CIA on CIA website at contact form.

I am waiting for CIA solve my problem.

People said Cointelpro, FBI, NSA, Homeland Security, Air Force, Navy.

I saw Chinese I thought China Neuro research with NSA, ROCKFELLER now I knew Taiwan, Rockefeller research and transgender CRIMINAL actions on my body.

CIA investigate I requested, let see if they do something.

President I don't know if he do something to stop these inhumanity, atrocity and amoral science secret performed tortured to citizens and other countries did to their people.

Dear CIA Director:

I would like to introduce myself to you, I am Vietnamese American, I fled out Viet Nam when Saigon surrendered to North Viet Nam in 1975, I resident in New Orleans, after Katrina hurricane I moved to Houston then sold house, moved to Horizon City, El Paso then sold house moved to Pennsylvania live with my son because lost from bought house, sold and moved several times, Targeted Individual.

I am a victim of Targeted Individual I just knew this after August 2010.

I was in fearfully, frighten and frustrated.

CIA in your profile or portfolio please let me know why I became target? Who I am? What fate, operation I was bad luck swift into that.

CIA DESTROYED MY ENTIRE LIFE!

At my age what reason CIA DESTROYED ME?

That operation continuing to my teenager then followed me until today.

I was under CIA secret research against my will, humiliated, tortured, mental terrible abused, killed, my health was paralyzed for 14 years, deprived life.

Since 2004 until today CIA used DEWs attacked to my brain, both subconscious, my woman body, my organs entire my physical body.

These technology damaged my beauty, my woman body, damaged my teeth, malfunction my organ system, harassed, high tech rape, disabled, illness, disease creation, harmful doing day and night.

Mind control sex terrible abused, neuro researched and applied control and robotized.

Perpetrators I saw Chinese and heard they were talking, who hired them or they joining research with CIA, NSA, Rockefeller.

I sent my complaint to CIA today the last one, I sent my complaint to NSA, Homeland Security, FBI, and Civil Court and Air-Force I requested investigation and settlement.

CIA responsibility for your wand of my fate life, please solve the amoral researched was burden on my life, my reputation, my life, health, my uniqueness, woman beauty and woman body, CIA pay settlements, stop TORTURE and SURVEILLANCE and official apology to me.

I am waiting for your solving this inhumanity research and atrocity crime applied research on me as Targeted Individuals.

Please investigate.

Respectfully,

Phiem Nguyen

June 14, 2019

They never stop, their weapon like metal stealth weapon attacked to my female sensitive part these days and today, they are devils, draculars.

They attacked to my legs all time I was in bathroom sink.

They shot to my head, hurtful my left back head near ear yesterday when I woke up I felt hurtful painful to my head.

My eye attacked to it and eye brawn.

My inside mouth their scalar 5G weapon jetted in, string in from my left cheek, I took mirror to fan it.

Runny nose, they created it, I was in unease when I don't have handkerchief or paper or Kleenex to wipe. I knew how to stop their remote nerve then yesterday morning their weapon attacked to my whole front head and face to create running nose, they remote sneezing in order runny nose, I could not understand these devils.

They are so terrible I could not know, Mind control is main reason.

June 15, 2019

Last night I went to bed and tried to be awakening but fell sleeping, I woke up or they woke me up after 2 hours, tried mind control me, invaded my subconscious and tweenlghtconscious.

They shot to my head several times hurtful painful.

At this time wake up I saw my left side mouth was attacking. Was swollen, I took pictures to show.

They attacked to my female, they tried to remote urine out.

I just release water but 10 minute later I needed to release water again I did not do it but after shower water released.

This morning I went outside exercise I knew they will embarrass me, they attacked to my both ears non stop to do mind control, after I finish walking water released. They followed me from their fusion center or office to see me in park.

They are sick devils Draculas

This evening I stood at kitchen sink to do dishes they attacked to my upper inside lip their weapon saw into my upper tissues continuous doing it, I felt soar, hurt like red pepper tough my inside lip, I took picture to prove.

June 17, 2019

Last night during time I was sleeping their weapon shot to my heart I felt pain at my heart they continued shot to my heart, I had to shield my heart, this evening I massage my feet they shot to my heart like last night they shot to my heart, they shot one time only.

Don't need to write daily routine attacking to my head, ears, neck behide my back head, stomach side, female, legs, feet.

June 18, 2019

They continued harmed me, the water they switched to their chemical, after I washed mouth, I felt something was wrong to my tange, another night I woke up my mouth smelt like fish sauce or salted worst smelt, few nights ago I woke up I saw my lower lip red swollen, inside mouth the layer skin tissues were pilled out?

That was reason they watched me every minute and second to harm me, these devils Chinese, Taiwan, Mossad CIA and Rockefeller did these things to me decades.

They kept attacking my left leg vein and my left near little toe to block my leg vein, they attacked to my thighs, harmful doing.

June 19, 2019

This morning I woke up I went to bathroom then came back my bedroom their collection smell bursted all my bedroom, their harmful chemical conceal under organic smell.

At this time 10: 30 p. m. I went back my bedroom all smell urine, my cooking food all inside my bedroom, their harmful chemical smell.

High tech rape my female all time.

They harmed my legs walking by attacked to my buttock bone join and vein thigh and my back vein feet.

My back shoulder vein and bone attacked to it harmed my arms.

My leg bone shot to it.

I took pictures to show.

June 20, 2019

They attacked to my left back head behide ear, the vast area was hurtful painful for days. They implanted their material, chip at my left side head they wanted to listen my thought. Don't need to listen I wrote it down here you can read it, devils.

June 21, 2019

THEY ASSAASINED ME RIGHT NOW

When I was in bed their stealth weapons attacked to my ankle bone painful hurtful my entire bone feet and ankle, I was sleeping then they woke me up to go to bathroom.

It is 1:09 a.m. I could not sleeping cause these devils tortured me, they are grouping people several places to do murdered me and harmed me with their weapons, their weapons stealth weapons shot to my buttock bone hurtful, painful, their weapon iterated my rectum nerve to remote wast out.

Their weapons went inside my female uterus, I cursed them their .5G jetted nano material inside my mouth and sticked to my throat.

They woke me up I went to bathroom then back my bed they attacked me, I could feel they are several groups of people to do these ill things, they tried to created cancer from dirty water with their harmful materials, their tech created disease inside my mouth I wrote that night they used 5 G technology jetted inside my mouth.

Medical Industrial Complex.

They shot to my left side head their weapon hurt inside my brain, hurtful painful my left side head, they tried to harm my feet for walking.

During time I was sleeping I don't know what they did to my head the right side I felt hurt pain inside my mainframe the whole day, listen to my thought and mind control from mainframe or they harm my vein, nerve and created stroke, they did these things to me when I was in El Paso also, I was fear for my head, my mainframe.

This afternoon I was in kitchen cooking they attacked my right side, their weapon shoot hard down inside to my brain from my top head, kept attacking my right side head mambrame

I am so resentful..

Medical Industrial Complex.

They are several groups people cruel actions.

They are killers, rapists, pedophile, tyrants, robbers and slender

June 23, 2019

They attacked and implanted foreigner materials or chips inside my head skull. It could be resulted from my mainframe, they did it to control, interfere and censored.

On June 21, 2019

I had to go to my appointment. These perpetrators hacked into my head to see to know what I was doing they Knew what I was saying which they expected I will do, my body was threatened werd heard their voice interfered into my brain knew and saying.

I hate so much these robber mind and brain, these people from NSA CHINA, TIWAN and ROCKFELKER RESEARCH AND APPLIED.

THEY'VE TO STOP AND PAY TRILLION TO ME.

I was under torture sleeping that was programmed during time I was sleeping each night and read on smart phone.

They made me sleepy and fell to sleepy I could not do things I needed to do, blocked and deprived life.

This morning they attacked to my left side front head painful what they wanted? Created stroke?

They attacked to my left side heart

My left side shoulder back bone.

My neck,

My Female, my legs and feet.

June 24, 2019

Yesterday morning I woke up I felt my hand hurtful I saw this cone at my hand this is coupable, I took picture to show.

Yesterday evening they attacked to my feet when I was at bathroom sink brushing teeth, it could be nucleus weapon.

My mouth their weapon inside my upper lip to implant their damage tissues into my lip tissues, they tried to damage my lip.

Yesterday afternoon I was using Rife machine during this time they used 5G to attacked inside my mouth to damaged my lip tissues and they attacked to my throat, my voice was changed I had difficult to talk.

Their 5G was using hacked to my phone and they hacked to electric also to Rife machine.

They tried to damaged me, sabotaged me,distracted me and tried to change me to man since 2007 until today, they damaged my woman body, their weapon destroyed beautiful feminine on my body.

My beauty distracted since 2004 until today.

This morning I woke up my head was heavy with their occupied the whole night invaded into my head, my brain.

Right now it is 6:04 a.m. they bursted their smell they store my urine smell but their harmful chemical to my nose.

This afternoon their steal weapons attacked to my behind left leg vein painful they harm my leg walking.

I am resentful each minute, I wanted trillion pay for my woman body, my beauty, my uniqueness, my reputation, my dignity, my life, my financial deprived.

June 27, 2019

I was busy to enter diary but don't think they stop.

Their weapon went inside mouth and my upper lip to damage tissues my upper lip, their plasma weapon cut to my upper lip I could feel the cut and I saw the dented line at my upper lip.

They attacked to my leg, behind leg vein. their stealth weapon pinned to my behind leg vein, they wanted to harm my walking.

My leg and feet their scalar weapon attacked from feet up to thighs.

They attacked to my head during time sleeping at night to injury my brain, vulnerable brain condition.

They attacked to my top head. front head, ears, eyes, neck, back, buttock bones.

This morning I was at toilet seat their weapon attacked to my stomach then at bathroom sink they attacked to my stomach and my lower abdomen painful, these day they attacked to my lower abdomen several times.

My leg picture on June -19-2019 with their pin shot compared to today my leg picture, readers can see harmful doing to me.

June 29, 2019

This morning I woke up with my front head under their tortured and harmed during the time I was sleeping, they attacked shot to my back head near ear went to inside brain.

Back and front head they assassined, my head was in painful and unease.

Their weapon shot to my heart this morning when I was in bathroom, my female constantly harass.

My hand and arm harmed bone and vein.

Attacked to my intestine, back lung, my legs and feet.

I am angry, fed up and I am so tired.

July 1, 2019

Last night when I went to bed to start sleeping I could feel they are several groups waiting sleeping they will do something on me.

Last night their weapon attacked to my left thigh when I was in bed to for I am start sleeping, they were constantly attacked to my feet and leg up to thigh.

This morning I woke up my left arm hurtful painful what they did during sleeping?

Dreamed other dream or inserted dream to do mind control.

What they did to my right arm, I just feel it but don't see it, I will take picture to show.

These days since weeks they attacked to my lower abdomen, today I was at kitchen sink and in bathroom sink they attacked to my lower abdomen, their weapon cut into it, my uterus? My bladder? Painful.

They are constantly attacked to my female day and night.

They are so terrible evils devils.

They are conquerors.

July 4, 2019

Last night when I woke up or they woke me up to hurry to go to bathroom then I came back my bedroom, I just step inside bathroom they shot to my stomach hurtful painful several hours later still.

This afternoon I do dishes at kitchen sink they attacked me nonstop, terrible.

Then later afternoon they attacked to my stomach intestine.

In the evening harass my female.

July 5, 2019

Last night during time I was sleeping their scalar weapon attacked to my both feet, I asked why they are so evil so devil and so coward, I could not imagine how suffer people if they rule!

They attacked to my leg, feet, ears, head, they never stop.

My female they were continuing harass day and night.

I needed seize power to stop, help me God Universe Sun

July 6, 2019

Last night their weapon scalar weapon attacked to my feet all night, harmed my feet.

This morning inside my bathroom their laser attacked to my vein thighs, they harmed my legs.

Afternoon their weapon attacked to my left side back lung, their weapon attacked to my stomach intestine place.

Female harass.

July 10, 2019

Yedterday their weapon kept shooting to my knee when I was doing dishes, my knee pain, hurt for walking.

Their weapon kept shooting to my feet when I was at kitchen sink and in bathroom sink even sat at toilet, they harm my feet walking.

Last night and the night before their scalar weapon kept attacking my feet during I was sleeping all night, they harmed my feet for walking.

This morning in bathtub they twisted my vein leg.

I am under these pedephile everyday why don't arrest them?

I am resentful.

At kitchen their stealth weapon shot to my right side breast.

Their weapon attacked to my back from my neck to lungs at kitchen isle.

Their weapons irritated my rectum, they are sick devils.

Their weapon shot to my stomach.

Their weapon attacked me from neck to lung whenever I sat at my bed.

July 11, 2019

What they did to my bladder during the time I was sleeping?

This morning I felt pain two both side my lower abdomen, what they tried to do, they wanted urine pouring out?

They are devils.

This morning they attacked to my female, harass, high tech raped, they are pedophile, why don't arrest them?

They attacked to my back head, back ear.

Their weapon picked to my left side lung I could feel the 2 inches circle hole this kind of weapon they used to dig hole at my buttock in order to get through my buttock to reach to my buttock bone.

They were constantly vibrated my whole lung back from neck to lung.

What they tried to do to my lung?

These perpetrators hacked into my phone to delete my note sentences I wrote down what they killed me.

They hacked into my computer deleted all videos I recorded their weapons attacked me.

They are conquerors.

July 13, 2019

It is 3:38 a.m. they woke me up with their scalar entire my feet attacking to harm my feet bone, they constantly attacked to my legs and feet to harm my feet walking.

They are cruel evils, devils.

Their device setting inside my bedroom or their weapon transmitted smell inside my bedroom to harm me, harm my health, itchy tonight

Yesterday afternoon their weapon attacked to my lower abdomen, their weapon kept posing attacked painful, I don't have extra hand to fight back, I was so angry to talk about their cruel action.

I saw the trace black pin at my right side lower abdomen I tried to took picture but could not.

July 14, 2019

I don't know what they did to my head during time I was sleeping, this morning I woke up I did not shield my head and stomach, it was surprised me.

They attacked to my head front head tried to create stroke.

They tried to attacked to my feet, legs, thigh leg bone harmed my walking.

My rectum their technology did something at my rectum

June 12, 2019

This night I wrote letter to send to CIA, CIA and Science did these terrible thing to my life, this is letter I email to CIA on CIA website at contact form.

I am waiting for CIA solve my problem.

People said Cointelpro, FBI, NSA, Homeland Security, Air Force, Navy.

I saw Chinese I thought China Neuro research with NSA, ROCKFELLER now I knew Taiwan, Rockefeller research and transgender CRIMINAL actions on my body.

CIA investigate I requested, let see if they do something.

President I don't know if he do something to stop these inhumanity, atrocity and amoral science secret performed tortured to citizens and other countries did to their people.

Dear CIA Director:

I would like to introduce myself to you, I am Vietnamese American, I fled out Viet Nam when Saigon surrendered to North Viet Nam in 1975, I resident in New Orleans, after Katrina hurricane I moved to Houston then sold house, moved to Horizon City, El Paso then sold house moved to Pennsylvania live with my son because lost from bought house, sold and moved several times, Targeted Individual.

I am a victim of Targeted Individual I just knew this after August 2010.

I was in fearfully, frighten and frustrated.

CIA in your profile or portfolio please let me know why I became target? Who I am? What fate, operation I was bad luck swift into that.

CIA DESTROYED MY ENTIRE LIFE!

At my age what reason CIA DESTROYED ME?

That operation continuing to my teenager then followed me until today.

I was under CIA secret research against my will, humiliated, tortured, mental terrible abused, killed, my health was paralyzed for 14 years, deprived life.

Since 2004 until today CIA used DEWs attacked to my brain, both subconscious, my woman body, my organs entire my physical body.

These technology damaged my beauty, my woman body, damaged my teeth, malfunction my organ system, harassed, high tech rape, disabled, illness, disease creation, harmful doing day and night.

Mind control sex terrible abused, neuro researched and applied control and robotized.

Perpetrators I saw Chinese and heard they were talking, who hired them or they joining research with CIA, NSA, Rockefeller.

I sent my complaint to CIA today the last one, I sent my complaint to NSA, Homeland Security, FBI, and Civil Court and Air-Force I requested investigation and settlement.

CIA responsibility for your wand of my fate life, please solve the amoral researched was burden on my life, my reputation, my life, health, my uniqueness, woman beauty and woman body, CIA pay settlements, stop TORTURE and SURVEILLANCE and official apology to me.

I am waiting for your solving this inhumanity research and atrocity crime applied research on me as Targeted Individuals.

Please investigate.

Respectfully,

Phiem Nguyen

June 14, 2019

They never stop, their weapon like metal stealth weapon attacked to my female sensitive part these days and today, they are devils, draculars.

They attacked to my legs all time I was in bathroom sink.

They shot to my head, hurtful my left back head near ear yesterday when I woke up I felt hurtful painful to my head.

My eye attacked to it and eye brawn.

My inside mouth their scalar 5G weapon jetted in, string in from my left cheek, I took mirror to fan it.

Runny nose, they created it, I was in unease when I don't have handkerchief or paper or Kleenex to wipe. I knew how to stop their remote nerve then yesterday morning their weapon attacked to my whole front head and face to create running nose, they remote sneezing in order runny nose, I could not understand these devils.

They are so terrible I could not know, Mind control is main reason.

June 15, 2019

Last night I went to bed and tried to be awakening but fell sleeping, I woke up or they woke me up after 2 hours, tried mind control me, invaded my subconscious and tweenlghtconscious.

They shot to my head several times hurtful painful.

At this time wake up I saw my left side mouth was attacking. Was swollen, I took pictures to show.

They attacked to my female, they tried to remote urine out.

I just release water but 10 minute later I needed to release water again I did not do it but after shower water released.

This morning I went outside exercise I knew they will embarrass me, they attacked to my both ears non stop to do mind control, after I finish walking water released. They followed me from their fusion center or office to see me in park.

They are sick devils Draculas

This evening I stood at kitchen sink to do dishes they attacked to my upper inside lip their weapon saw into my upper tissues continuous doing it, I felt soar, hurt like red pepper tough my inside lip, I took picture to prove.

August 22, 2019

Just moment at kitchen sink I could feel their weapons shot and went inside tissues of my left mouth side, lip and cheek, distracted my appearance, degraded my natural beauty.

I took pictures to show.

Today I started new diary because yesterday I prepared to arrange book but accident I lost all diary from December 2, 2018.

August 24, 2019

They never stop.

Yesterday they very strong shot to my right side head then continued attacked to my right side head, killed? Harmed? Immoral harmed?

They did what they knew.

Today worst attacking to my female, their weapons attacked to my female constantly long hours I saw black color at my under-ware and paper.

Their weapons attacked to my rectum to tortured, malfunction my bowel movement.

I was so angry!

August 25, 2019

Their scalar weapon attacked to my stomach, intestine both side and at my belly for hours when I started eat my meal at kitchen, I took picture to show, what they tried to harm?

August 27, 2019

Today and yesterday they attached to my left side breast painfully, what they tried to do to my breast, my breast they damaged it since 2007 until today, it made me more angry each day.

August 28, 2019

Today at kitchen they attacked to my right under knee leg, they twisted my vein and did something to bone leg, don't know why they tried to harm my walking, coward fear to show their faces.

Attacked to my right ear through nerves, sex nerves.

Attacked to my female, their weapon attacked to my female sides, what they tried to do now?

Since 2007, they damaged my female and my breasts.

Then their scalar weapon vanished my beautiful feminine on my woman body.

Their weapon attacked to my left lung, they vibrated the whole back lung and muscles.

After dinner they attacked to my stomach created upset stomach.

Their weapon shot to my top head when I sat on toilet seat.

They are devils and mental illness bad luck if they still on this earth.

They are my enemies.

August 30, 2019

This morning I woke up I don't know what they did during time I was sleeping my right thumb hurtful.

At kitchen attacked to my female painful shot into my female side and female form near to female sensitive then continuing attacked to my female tortured, I could not live the life line this for decades with their weapons tortured.

I wanted them be death penalty and their technology be destroyed all.

Inside bathroom their weapons shot to my head, why they so devil?

These perpetrators are Chinese intelligent research with Taiwanese do associate with transgender group research and applied.

I don't know if CIA worked with them or allowed them to do, NSA, ROCKEFELLER and Military research.

I want to know who is Alluminity?

Who is MASON? Who is Deep State?

I don't have change to read the book Dan Brown.

September 2, 2019

Last night during I was sleeping they harmed my shoulder bone, I woke up with uncomfortable their weapons attacked to my two shoulders and butter cup bones, I had to shield it.

This morning I took picture to show their weapon attacked to my shoulders, they harmed my hands working, moving.

During I took shower their weapons attacked to my thighs painful inside flesh, they created cancer.

Outside on my legs they created cancer on my skin, the black dots on my under knee legs.

All night invaded subconscious to harm my life with their mind control weapon inserted dreams then woke me up, I went back sleep then created another dream. Humiliated inside my subconscious, inability life or deprived life.

Urine sex torture all night every night.

They are so terrible evils.

September 3, 2019

Last night their inserted dreams mind control, invaded my brain and mind.

After sleeping our mind, brain and body refreshed.

Their victim like me woke up heavy mind brain occupied, body exhausted, felt body pain.

Urine sex they never stop.

September 5, 2019

Today they are constantly attacked to my female side, these devils should be killed.

I am resentful.

They are my annemies.

September 8, 2019

Yesterday I found out my left side sole their pin the whole corn they created because I felt hurtful.

This morning I woke up I felt my left feet bone near the corn was pain, they harmed during the time I was sleeping.

Today at kitchen their food smell I thought neighbor bake cake and food but I don't know it was from smell affected my central nervous system or it was from their weapon attacked to me via iPhone.

Coinstelpro did these sick ill science to destroy my life in USA, CIA did sick ill thing to destroy my life in Viet Nam.

Justice Department recorded US Government did sick ill thing to me innocence or recorded victim did it?

When I was in Houston I read article about scary thing what they record on people we should check.

I search for my record, I paid fee by my credit card, they will send record to my email but I wait for a month I did not receive it, I waited for my credit card statement if they charge, no they did not charge.

I wish for someone check my record then tell me.

I sold my house moved to El-Paso later someone posted on search engine my name, that I am molest child, I was shocked.

They held down my head to created sick ill then they observed their sick ill for their research and nourish their amoral sex, they said that I did it, they did not do it, sick ill Devil cowards.

Do they remembered Harvey Comet to destroy this earth at that sick ill time.

Now Government and executed of Government did these sick ill thing to people, you have responsibility to official apologize, settlement and stop this evil doing to innocent people.

I, today requested Government should issue apology official letter to me to prove to public and my family generations.

They are conquerors they destroyed people, harmed and black mail then black list people, they controlled.

Now I wanted all these hippocrits are on blacklist and criminal not victims.

September 9, 2019

Yesterday they shot to my right head hurtful painful all day yesterday the night and today, I place natural against their weapons and massaged my head, they are so terrible evils.

At bathroom they shot to my under knee legs, ankle and remote pain at my sole.

This morning at kitchen they still attacked my head, back head, ears, back, lower abdomen, my legs, feet and female.

September 10, 2019

Last night their inserted dream to humiliate me and did mind control also. They waited for me to go sleeping then raped my female with their weapons to do sick sex, Incest mind control, these China and Chinese associate with ill sick science.

September 12, 2019

Last night I was in bed they are several groups surrounding me to attack and harass rape.

They shot to my mouth side and lip, shot to my female same weapons they shot to my side mouth, I took picture to show.

Their weapons jetted itchy to my arm I don't know what chemical or disease, after my reading done I had alcohol wipered I saw black color on paper towel.

My head and ears assaulted attacking. This morning my head near right ear is hurful painful.

I woke up this morning terrible hurt pain from my head to entire my body, I saw dented in at my forefront I forgot to take picture it,

Day and night tortured, harmed and inserted their dreams to do mind control.

September 13, 2019

Last night I was in bed to rest their weapons shot under my left breast went inside my heart bosom I felt the strange I never have before in my life, I don't know how to describe for understand the things was happened.

My bosom was looked like expanding, strange felt could not explain then went to my back hurtful painful with strange thing I never had that before.

I shielded my heart and under my breast but it was continuing pain and vulnerable heart, later I went to bathroom, I was tired and my heart beated, I knew they created my heart failure.

Medical Industrial Complex Research, Military Industrial Complex Research, BIO-TECHNO-TERRORISTS PERFORMED.

I knew they are same group because they did to my heart and lung when I was in Horizon City El Paso. They assassined me.

I went on my therapy to cure.

This morning I observed my breast chest and back, I only see under my left breast the dot, I could not see my back lung.

I took pictures to show.

This morning I woke up with my feet scalar weapon attacked.

Then this morning I felt my right head was under their chip in or they inserted their material into my brain or my skull head to do mind control or they took out my brain tissues.

At kitchen they continue attacked to my head.

From microwave control attacking to my head created dizziness.

At bathroom their weapons painful shot to my right shoulder bone affected to my arm nerves.

Tortured every minutes.

September 14, 2019

Last night I was sleeping their weapons attacked to my right side back lung at the arm bone moving connection, it was so painful I woke up then I shield it.

This morning I woke up I still feel pain and moving arm painful too, exercised to release.

This harmful to my nerves and vein.

They attacked to my backlung arm bone connection again at kitchen and control my vein and nerves.

Here in bedroom I sat at chair, their weapons attacked to my female raped high tech raped and attacked to my both ears to do mind control sex, they attacked to my back head and neck to harm my nervous system and nerves.

During night and yesterday night I heard they were at my head bed or neighbor house talking, these Chinese and Mossad did these things to my head, they created stroke from my head.

When I was in kitchen their weapon knocked to my right side head terrible strange hurt inside my brain, they did harm Inside my brain, I could feel my head they blocked brain inside my head, I felt strange blocked affected my brain, my eating and my food testing, fed up testing.

I heard they were laughing.

My back joining arm bone and spine cord were attacked to it to harm my back bone and arm bone.

They are criminals, assassined, tortured, raped, damaged, diseases, illness, abnormal, malfunction, damaged, distracted, sabotaged, abused, impoverished, deprived life.

They are my enemies.

September 15, 2019

Their weapon attacked to my head, neck, back lung arm bone, vibrated my lungs, scalar attacked my legs.

Everyday and every minute second my body and my brain on their computer screen to attack, harass, tortured, killed, harmed.

Their weapon tried to attacked to my heart, they knew my heart soar.

Killers you should be destroyed and your technology.

September 17, 2919

Last night their weapon attacked to my female, legs and their knife weapon attacked to my inside lower abdomen what they cut? What they harm?

I was so angry with their damaging technology and their secretly did on my body day and night harmful doing and tortured, abused, sabotaged on my physical body, my health, organs, my head, brain, my uniqueness, my life, I was in more anger each day, angry, distress since 2004.

They pabdicated us all from inside house and from our body to brain to mind to privacy.

No one do anything to stop them.

God lift your finger to dust their technology and prison them all.

This morning I woke up with my arm back bone hurtful and two nights continuous their weapon attacked to my arm backbone hurtful, harmed my hand for working.

Their weapons was through my iPhone to attacked me when I hold phone to use or their weapons outside to shot to my thumbs.

I had experienced attacking from iPhone, they used phone to attack like from computer attacking.

Two night ago during time I was sleeping they attacked to my head affected to my eye,

Line glaucoma.

My eye had the light scar when I did sun practicing, they might be did something or eye medicine o took I did not see the floating scar for awhile then now it was back with their scar creation.

Harmful doing every they could on my health, my brain and my body.

This evening at kitchen their weapons attacked to my head, assassined me day and night.

September 18, 2019

Last night rapist team their weapons raped my female then their weapon pin went inside my rectum then went up to my throat.

I fought with them every minute day and night since 2004 until today.

People can see their dangerous technology weapons.

This morning I woke up with my left side back pain at kidney, what they did during time I was sleeping?

After I took shower I went back bedroom what they did to my heart I felt heart was harmed and I felt tired.

They are criminals I was under these atrocious assassined, harassed, raped, sabotaged, damaged, illness, disease, disabled creation, tortured, abused, degraded, distracted, harmed and deprived life.

September 19, 2019

Last night they killed me.

They woke me up after urine sex rape during time I was sleeping every night, each time I have to hurry to go to bathroom and water their technology forced out.

Then I went back my bedroom and started return sleeping again. I felt tired I did not know reason and I waited to see what will happen then I felt my left breast was under pressure by weapon to hurt and pain and continuing expand from my left breast to my under arm that was my hear arteries, my heart was in Invaded to create heart attack, I was immediately shield my heart, they were continuing attack my heart and I continued shielding my heart long as they stopped.

These Chinese researchers were invaded my physical body from brain to feet from inside to skin researched and applied research since 2007 I had lived in Houston TX.

Their invisible technology weapon and their hidden hands were freely to do what they wanted to do on my head, brain and my entire physical body.

How can I fight them back?

Government don't do anything to stop but continuing along their technology weapons developed.

I prayed to God lift your finger to destroy their weapons. Jail or death penalty them all.

September 20, 2019

Last night I was in my bedroom their weapons shot to my heart where my heart was harmed pain, their weapon posed at that place, I did not shield my heart let see what they wanted do next, they kept shooting until they don't want to continue.

This morning I took pictures to show.

Then their weapons needled pinned into my upper lip I felt pain but I did not shield my lip as I usually do however my lip was distracted, they needled then their weapon posed to my lip both side left and right, they distracted my lip until they stop.

This morning I took pictures my lips, my mouth to show.

Today at kitchen their weapon attacked to my lungs their weapon like stealth attacked directed to my lungs, severe hurt pain, they harmed my lungs.

I could not take picture or see what they did to my lungs.

Their stealth weapons attacked to female form inside flesh.

God lift your finger destroy them all and their technology, they are devils.

Just moment in bathroom their weapon jetted in vaccines, I was surprised when I saw blood bleeding.

What diseases or chips they jetted in.

I took pictures to show

September 21, 2019

Just moment in bathroom their weapon jetted into my left hand I just saw the big red dot, I wiped it out but it is still on my hand, I don't know what they tried to do, diseases, chips or something else.

I took pictures to show.

September 24, 2019

I woke up to go to bathroom my head was so hurtful painful, what they did during time I was sleeping?

I felt tired.

September 25, 2019

This morning I woke up I saw my I saw my left foot was frighten me I took picture to show. They stole my tissues, flesh.

My head recently attacked to my head to create stroke then continue attacking to my head everyday, my heart tiring, my test was lost, my digest was in trouble, these things were don from my brain.

My heart was assassined processing I was noted and described it few days ago.

They attacked to my throat, attacked to my ovary place, this, they were constantly attacked for years since 2007 everyday until they malfunction my urine system and bowel movement system, they loosen it on everyday they did before.

My ears were constantly attacked to it to do mind controlled.

My ear at earring places their weapon attacked to it places like pliers plied into it terrible hurt, they kept doing several times when I had live in Horizon, TX.

They changed it shape to thinner and smaller they stole my ear tissues, I took pictures to show.

Everyday anger day for decades.

Now it is 11:24 p.m. Eastern time.

I was in my bed, their weapons attacked to my stomach to assassin me, I felt stomach ache, I thought it was from onion sour apple cider vinegar I ate when my stomach was empty.

I needed to turn off phone charging and go to bathroom before sleeping, I went to bathroom I don't feel stomach ache, I knew immediately that was perpetrators, these people were from nanomafia and China intelligent research because they did this thing to me before, I had experience terrible pain they did to inserted pain into brain, I thought I could die at that time, other TI said her husband died during week they did to me.

Just few days ago science said measure pain from brain to know how level pain people was.

No one prosecute them, Bioethics Committees TIs testimony don't stop them, they kept going on like nobody can do anything to them.

They are aliens? Invisible weapons and invisible hands and faces, freely to do what they wanted to do day and night to people like me to destroy day by day, every minute, every second and every centimeter on our bodies from head to toes to sole, from inside to skin. Invaded our privacy from brain to house, to bedroom to bathroom.

Frankenstein.

September 26, 2019

All night their weapon posed to my stomach created pain inside my stomach, created cancer? Dr Rife is helping people.

I went back Dr. Rife therapy then I was falling sleeping I woke up this morning free of urine sex torture and forced out water.

I felt something at my stomach because I did not shield.

I took picture to show.

Printed in the United States
By Bookmasters